Jeff Lahr

REGULAR BAPTIST PRESS
1300 North Meacham Road
Schaumburg, Illinois 60173-4888

*Dedicated to Jack and Julie Dove,*
*true Christian friends*

MUSIC OF THE MANGER

Regular Baptist Press
Schaumburg, Illinois



Printed in U.S.A.


ISBN: 0-87227-183-8

# Table of Contents

# Christmas Play Organizational Chart

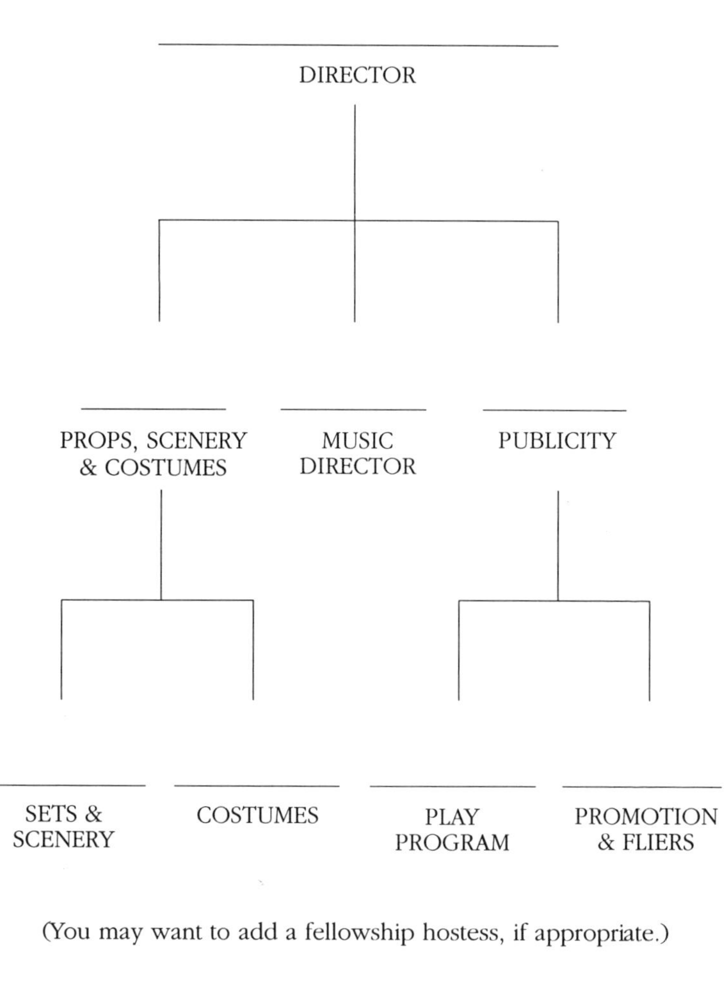


(You may want to add a fellowship hostess, if appropriate.)

**REHEARSAL DATES AND TIMES**

______________________________

______________________________

## A Note from the Author to the Director

Directing a Christmas program is always a challenge, especially if it is your first time! If this is your first time, praise God! You have a terrific opportunity to evangelize and minister to a large number of people.

Being in charge of the Christmas program can result in great blessings—or headaches. Much of the outcome depends upon your attitude as director. One of the director's most important jobs is to set the tone for the preparation of the program. Approach it with enthusiasm and a keen sense of mission, and you will receive remarkable rewards!

You will want to concentrate in the following areas:

**Preparation.** Being prepared makes your job as director much easier. It means knowing the program thoroughly and making decisions thoughtfully beforehand so you won't have to make hasty decisions later.

One area of preparation is delegation. Producing a program involves different aspects, and it is difficult for one person to take responsibility for them all. By sharing the tasks with others, you will feel less stress, different details will receive greater attention, and others will get to participate in this ministry. The chart on page 4 gives you some ideas of jobs that you can delegate.

Another aspect of preparation is organization. Plan a rehearsal schedule and a time line for completing the different tasks. Check it out with your pastor, print it and give copies to the participants. Include it on your church's calendar as well.

**Practice.** Start early. October seems like a long time before Christmas, but by having most of the rehearsals during Sunday School, you will need just six or seven practices. This number should be plenty for the departments. The actors from the Primary Department will need more rehearsals. A few extra Saturday-morning practices should be enough. One final practice should include everyone in the program. At that time, different groups can be fitted for costumes or rehearse songs, while others practice their parts on stage. The practice should conclude with a final and complete run-through.

**Patience.** This will be the first experience on stage for many young people—be prepared for some surprises! Some of them may not have the level of commitment you expect; encourage them and pray that this experience will further their Christian walk. Some frustrations come as you work the bugs out—it's all part of the creative process.

**Prayer.** God is glorified in the entire process of preparing for the program—not just the actual performance. Use this preparation as a time to get to know your church's young people and to share your love of God with them.

The Christmas program is one of the best-attended services of the year at many churches. Take advantage of this fact. A program gives you great opportunity to share the blessings God has bestowed upon you. Suggest to your pastor that a dessert fellowship take place afterward. (Be sure to delegate that job!)

Ask God for guidance. He will bless your efforts.

## Production Notes

**Staging.** Staging requirements for *Music of the Manger* are simple. For the contemporary scenes (scenes 1 and 4), the set represents a living room. This setting can be portrayed realistically with lots of props or symbolically with just a chair or two. After scene 1, the actors can move the contemporary set props as they leave the stage. (If your youth group has shy members who do not want to perform, you may want to make them responsible for the set design and construction and for the scene changes.)

The manger scene can be a simple wooden stool or a bench. Drape a bed sheet, dyed or spray-painted in browns and grays, over a contemporary piece of furniture to represent wood and stone. Some churches construct a manger out of wood or painted cardboard, and some use an open (without walls) canopy-style manger made of dyed sheets.

**Costumes.** As with set design, costumes can be as

simple or elaborate as the director chooses. Many directors prefer to delegate the job of costuming to another creative adult in the church. The young children in the Preschool Department may dress in their "Sunday best" or in costumes representing different animals of the manger.

The children in the Primary Department portray the shepherds. Robes, sashes and headpieces made of bright cloth remnants make great costumes.

The students in the Junior Department represent the heavenly hosts. Because the Bible does not give a detailed physical description of angels, a great deal of imagination can be used in costuming them. But most people stick to the traditional white robes and tinsel or garland halos.

**The Performance.** Although *Music of the Manger* will be performed across the country, every performance will be different! Part of the reward of directing a play is to adapt a plan to meet the needs of your church family. It is not important if your church doesn't have a large stage, lights or a big budget. What is important, however, is that the program clearly presents the gospel message to the audience. Here are some ideas to help "get the message out":

• *Speaking:* Cast members should speak loudly, slowly and distinctly. Most understand the idea of speaking slowly and loudly, but they have trouble realizing the importance of good enunciation. Teach them to stretch the vowels and pronounce the consonants crisply as they use their performer's voice. Use a bit of silence to separate words and allow the audience to absorb the ideas. (Silence is an important but usually neglected tool on stage.)

In the dialogue, a dash (—) indicates a sudden break in speech, such as an interruption or an abrupt change in thought. Ellipses (…) indicate faltering speech caused by uncertainty, distress or confusion.

• *Blocking:* Blocking is the theatrical term for movement and placement of actors on the stage. Avoid having a lineup of actors simply volleying their lines back and forth. Instead, create depth by placing some actors near the front of the performing area and some near the rear. Give your actors a reason to move across stage and do something. Be careful that movement is not overdone or distracting.

• When actors narrate nativity scenes, they will do best if they have their parts well practiced but not necessarily memorized. They can perform either offstage using a microphone or onstage. If in front of the audience, they can read from their scripts, which should be inside choir folders. They should draw as little attention to themselves as possible.

## Characters

(In Order of Appearance)

Casting is flexible. Make this play fit the needs of your congregation!

Tim: A teen boy, Tim is eager to share the Christmas story by singing carols to neighbors.

Bobby: A humorous teen boy, Bobby is enthusiastic and impulsive.

Jessica: A typical teen girl, Jessica provides some thoughtful insight during the play.

Janice: The "spark plug" of the young people, Janice is both fun and sensitive.

All actors have about the same number of lines to memorize (with the part of Janice slightly shorter than the others). As the play is written, they "perform" in scenes 1 and 4 and narrate the nativity scenes (2 and 3) and the epilogue. Bobby and Jessica have the longer parts to narrate.

If you want a larger number of young people to participate in the program, you can give the narration parts to other speakers. Up to eight optional parts for speakers are written into the play: scene 2—optional speakers #1 and #2; scene 3—optional speakers #3 and #4; epilogue—optional speakers #5 through #8.

## Sunday School Departments

*Preschool* (children ages two through kindergarten-age): (Throughout the program the term "preschoolers" or "Preschool Department" will include children in kindergarten.) The preschoolers help set the manger scene by carrying cardboard cutouts of animals and singing several songs, such as "Away in a Manger," "Little Baby in the Manger, 'I Love you' " and "Silent Night." They have no speaking parts.

*Primary* (grades one through three): Primary-age children play the part of the shepherds and can be creatively costumed with slightly altered bathrobes and other easily found pieces of wardrobe. The shepherds sing two songs: "Angels' Chorus" and the "Christmas Song." The members of the Primary Department recite the poem "Like a Lamb." The poem has six speaking parts.

*Junior* (grades four through six): The students in the Junior Department represent some shepherds and the angels. They sing two songs: "Angels' Chorus" and the "Christmas Song." They have ten solo speaking parts. Three parts consist of two lines of Scripture each. The group recites the poems "A Flock without a Shepherd" and "Angels' Answer"—with seven solo speaking parts and with the whole group reciting each last line.

*All Departments:* The entire group recites John 3:16 and sings "Unfinished Symphony" during the epilogue.

". . . But be filled with the Spirit; Speaking to yourselves
in psalms and hymns and spiritual songs,
singing and making melody in your heart to the Lord."
Ephesians 5:18, 19

# Music of the Manger
## Scene 1

*At curtain rise: A simple living room set. Three friends are preparing to go caroling. They are bundling up in jackets and scarves.*

TIM: Are we about ready to go?

BOBBY: I wonder where Janice is. She should be here by now.

JESSICA: She'll be here. She wouldn't miss it.

BOBBY: She loves to sing Christmas carols.

TIM: We all do!

*JESSICA and TIM step together to "draw" a caroling scene.*

JESSICA: You bet. It's great going out on a frosty night—

TIM: Knocking on your neighbors' doors—

BOBBY *(rather rudely sticks his head between them) (in a greedy voice):* —And people give you cookies.

TIM, JESSICA *(Both turn to glare at Bobby.) (in unison):* Not yet!

*JESSICA and TIM get in the dreamy mood again, as they recreate the caroling scene in their minds.*

JESSICA: And then they open the door—

BOBBY *(interrupting them again):* —And people give you cookies.

TIM, JESSICA *(sharply and in unison):* Not yet!

TIM: And they look so surprised!

BOBBY: And people give you cookies.

TIM, JESSICA *(sharply and in unison):* Not yet!

JESSICA: And when you start to sing, they look so pleased.

TIM: They get this faraway look in their eyes.

BOBBY: And people give you cookies.

TIM, JESSICA *(sharply and in unison):* Not yet!

JESSICA: And for just a minute, they stop all the Christmas hustle and bustle and listen—really listen—to songs about our Savior's birth.

TIM: Jesus, the Christ Child.

*After a brief moment of thoughtful reflection, JESSICA and TIM begin to tease BOBBY.*

JESSICA: And then . . .

*As BOBBY'S excitement mounts, TIM and JESSICA on both sides of him step closer and closer.*

BOBBY: Yeah . . . Yeah . . .

TIM: And then . . .

BOBBY: Yeah . . . Go on, go on!

*Slight pause ensues, and then TIM and JESSICA on each side of BOBBY practically shout.*

TIM, JESSICA *(in unison):* And then they give you cookies!

*A moment of silence passes before BOBBY reacts.*

BOBBY: Is that all you guys think about? Food?

JESSICA: Of course it isn't just the food. It's the smiles!

TIM: And Janice usually has the biggest smile of all.

BOBBY: So where is she?

TIM: Maybe she's practicing her smile.

JESSICA: She'll be here. She wouldn't miss Christmas caroling; it's a tradition.

TIM: I can't understand it. She was supposed to be here a long time ago.

BOBBY: And she's usually early. *(pause)* Maybe she's not coming.

TIM: Not coming!

JESSICA: Impossible! She'll be here.

TIM: Can you imagine caroling without Janice?

*BOBBY sits down disappointedly.*

BOBBY: Caroling without Janice? It just wouldn't be the same.

TIM: That would be like Christmas without caroling.

BOBBY: Maybe we should call the whole thing off.

JESSICA: That's ridiculous. She'll walk through that door, bundled up against the cold—ready to sing!

BOBBY: Yeah, that's right. With that big ol' grin of hers.

TIM *(looking out the window):* Hey, look! Here she comes now.

BOBBY: She'll walk right through that door with so much excitement she'll hardly be able to contain herself.

JESSICA: She'll be coming through that door any minute. . . .

*The three friends gather around the door waiting for her, frozen in a pose of excitement. JANICE enters, but she walks in gloomily.*

JANICE *(glumly):* Hi guys.

*JANICE walks past the three other characters who are still "frozen" in eager anticipation. One by one they "unfreeze" and become gloomy too.*

JESSICA: There she is, Miss Enthusiasm.

BOBBY, TIM *(in unison):* What's the matter with you?

JANICE: Nothing . . . I'm fine.

*TIM approaches JANICE and places an arm around her, being overly supportive.*

TIM: Janice, Janice. This is it! This is the night we go caroling.

BOBBY: Our Christmas tradition.

JANICE: Sure. I guess we might as well go.

JESSICA: Janice, you're acting so strange. What's the matter? This isn't like you.

JANICE: I was just *thinking*. . . .

BOBBY *(to JESSICA):* You're right, that *isn't* like her.

TIM: So what's the problem?

JANICE: It isn't a problem . . . really. *(pause)* It's just that we enjoy Christmas so much.

BOBBY *(sounding very confident as though he has solved the problem):* Oh, I get it. Now I understand the problem. . . . All this enjoyment . . . you find it depressing! *(Realizing what he just said doesn't make a bit of sense, he pauses and scratches his head.)* Maybe you'd better explain it one more time . . . *(points to the others)* so they'll understand too.

JANICE: No, listen. We love Christmas. But what is it that we love so much?

JESSICA: We love to celebrate our Savior's birth.

*Their excitement begins to build.*

JANICE: Right. We celebrate. But how do we do that?

TIM: Oh, a lot of different ways. We share gifts. We decorate our houses. We attend special church services—

BOBBY: —We put on Christmas plays at church.

*All moan, good-naturedly.*

JESSICA: And we sing.

JANICE: Exactly. We sing! Music is such an important part of our Christmas celebration.

TIM: You can hear Christmas music everywhere: at church, on the radio, in the stores.

BOBBY: We go caroling too. We celebrate by singing.

JESSICA: If we don't quit talking, we won't have time to carol tonight.

JANICE: No, wait a minute. Can you imagine Christmas without music?

TIM: No music?

BOBBY: You mean no songs, no hymns, no Christmas carols?

JESSICA: It wouldn't be the same.

JANICE: Exactly. Imagine that first Christmas eve. Mary and Joseph are alone in the manger. It must have seemed so quiet and empty. No song. No celebration. No music. Just Mary and Joseph all alone. It seems so depressing. That's why I was a little sad.

BOBBY: They weren't exactly alone. The animals were there.

JESSICA: And the shepherds. They came later.

TIM: And the angels.

JANICE: True. But no music. No Christmas carols.

JESSICA: No Christmas carols, perhaps. But there was music, and I'll bet it was a celebration of music. Jesus' birth was a time for celebrating, and I can't believe the Lord would have allowed it to be silent!

JANICE: It's hard to imagine.

JESSICA: Let's try. *(JESSICA pauses slightly, turns and addresses the audience.)* Let's use our imagination and listen for the music of the manger.

*Lights dim.*

## Scene 2

(Mary, Joseph, Preschoolers and Kindergartners)

*An empty manger scene stands on center stage. TIM and JANICE (or optional speakers #1 and #2) enter, standing to side of stage, and narrate, or they may narrate off-stage using a microphone. If the narrators perform in front of the audience, place the narration in choir folders. The narrators should then read the narration rather than recite it from memory.*

*To set the scene, an adult or teenager should sing "Righteous Child."*

# Righteous Child

Jeffery G. Lahr

21
crown of ag-o-ny. Born to die up - on Cal-v'ry's tree. Born to save us
21
25
from our sin, the Sav - ior of the world. Je - sus,
25
29
Sav - ior, Son of God. Ho - ly
29
33
in - fant, Righ - teous One.
33
37
37

41
41
45
In a crib of hu - mil - i - ty, sleeps the child de - i - ty—
45
49
Born to save hu - man - i - ty, the Sav - ior of the world.
49
53
Je - sus, Sav - ior, Son of God.
53
57
Ho - ly in - fant, Righ - teous One.
57

61
Je - sus, Sav - ior, Son of God.
61
65
Ho - ly in - fant, Righ - teous One.
65
69
69
73
73
77
77
8vb

*If speakers are miked, the instrumentalist may continue to play "Righteous Child" during the narration.*

*As TIM begins narration, MARY and JOSEPH walk slowly across the stage and sit in the manger scene.*

TIM: On that first Christmas, Joseph and Mary had traveled to Bethlehem to be taxed as commanded by the Roman governor. Mary was "great with child." They had traveled several days along the dusty road to the City of David.

JANICE: They were probably hot, tired and looking forward to a night's lodging. But the city was crowded with travelers, and they could find no room in the inn. Instead they found rest in a stable.

JANICE, TIM *(pause slightly and then in unison):* Their only company were the beasts of the field.

*Children from the Preschool Department enter. Some students carry cardboard cutouts of donkeys and sheep and place them in the manger scene. Children sing "Away in a Manger" (available in many hymnals) or "Little Baby in the Manger, 'I Love You'" (from* Preschoolers Sing and Say, *Regular Baptist Press, p. 11). After they sing, the children surround the manger scene (holding as still as possible) until the end of the narration.*

TIM: In this manger of humble birth, Jesus Christ became flesh and "dwelt among us."

JANICE: According to God's design, this was the time . . .

TIM: And this was the place . . .

JANICE, TIM *(in unison):* For His eternal plan to begin.

JANICE: Mary and Joseph alone in the stable.

TIM: It was truly a silent night.

*The children from the Preschool Department sing "Silent Night" (song found in hymnals).*

JANICE: The time had come for the song of salvation to begin. *(softly)* It started quietly, as soft as the song of a dove. *(louder)* But before the night was through, it would become—

TIM, JANICE *(triumphantly and in unison)*: —A symphony of celebration.

*TIM and JANICE (or optional narrators #1 & #2) exit with preschoolers.*

## Scene 3

The Shepherds (Primary Department)

*BOBBY and JESSICA (or optional speakers #3 and #4) enter.*

BOBBY: The music of the manger had begun! New voices came to announce the birth of the King.

BOBBY: "There were in the same country shepherds abiding in the field, keeping watch over their flock by night."

JESSICA: The angels would appear to them first.

*Shepherds from the Primary and Junior departments enter. The shepherds from the Primary Department recite "Like a*

*Lamb." Then all the shepherds "set up camp" in the performance area across from the manger.*

## Like a Lamb

(Primary Shepherds)

SPEAKER #1

Shepherds watching in the field,
Guarding all their master's sheep
From all danger they would shield.
From all risk, the flock they'd keep.

SPEAKER #2

Like a shepherd, Jesus cares
What we say and what we do,
Living lives to please our Savior.
Let me be His foll'wer, too.

SPEAKER #3

Little lambs must watch their actions
What they do and where they go.
At all times, in work and play,
Loving God should always show.

SPEAKER #4

Little lambs must watch their words
Guarding everything they say,
Have no time for hateful words
But always take the time to pray.

SPEAKER #5

Little lambs must guard their minds
Protecting them from sinful thought,
Growing up to be more kind
By learning lessons Jesus taught.

SPEAKER #6

Little lambs must always keep
In His promise, trusting sure,
Living lives to please the Shepherd,
Mind and body always pure.

BOBBY: But why did the angels appear first to the simple shepherds? Why didn't the angels share the good news with *all* the people of Bethlehem?

JESSICA: Perhaps the people of the city were too busy to hear the angels sing.

BOBBY: From their location on the hillsides near Bethlehem, maybe the shepherds could watch the people hustling and bustling all over the city.

JESSICA: From the fields, the shepherds may have shouted to the people of Bethlehem, but they were too busy—too busy for God.

BOBBY: The shepherds knew what Isaiah the prophet had written: "All we like sheep have gone astray; we have turned every-one to his own way."

JESSICA: The chosen people of God had become a flock without a shepherd.

*The shepherds from the Junior Department stand and recite the poem, "A Flock without a Shepherd." Four shepherds recite one stanza each, but all the shepherds from the Junior Department recite the last line of the stanza (printed in bold).*

## A Flock without a Shepherd

Shepherds' Lament

SPEAKER #1

As their eyes swept past the lights of the city,
Down the face of the shepherds fell tears of pity.
The people of Bethlehem had gone astray,
Everyone had gone his own way.
**A flock without a shepherd.**

SPEAKER #2

A shepherd was needed to lead and to guide
Within His protection, a place to hide.
But the people of Bethlehem had gone astray,
Everyone had gone his own way.
**A flock without a shepherd.**

SPEAKER #3

Forsaking a shepherd's protection and care
God's burden and will they did not share.
The people of Bethlehem had gone astray;
Everyone had gone his own way.
**A flock without a shepherd.**

SPEAKER #4

"Has He forsaken his people; do our cries go unheard?
Where is the Shepherd pledged in God's Word?"
In the field, the shepherds cry.
But the people of Bethlehem walk right by.
**A flock without a shepherd.**

JESSICA: "And, lo, the angel of the Lord came upon them, and the glory of the Lord shone round about them: and they were sore afraid."

*Six juniors enter as angels. They stand behind the shepherds. The shepherds turn, kneel and face the angels. The angels speak over the kneeling shepherds to the audience. They recite Luke 2:10–14.*

ANGEL #1: "Fear not: for, behold, I bring you tidings of great joy, which shall be to all people."

ANGEL #2: "For unto you is born this day in the city of David, a Saviour, [who] is Christ the Lord."

ANGEL #3: "And this shall be a sign unto you; Ye shall find the babe wrapped in swaddling clothes, lying in a manger."

*Angels recite "Angel's Answer." Three speakers recite one stanza each. The entire group recites the final lines (printed in bold).*

## Angels' Answer

ANGEL #4

"Fear not," cry the angels, "fear not.
For born tonight is the One you sought."
Promised through prophecy in God's Holy Word,
He that is born shall be the Good Shepherd.
**A shepherd for His people.**

ANGEL #5

'Tis true the flock has been scattered,
But preserve your faith unshattered.
The promise relies not on what we say or do
But on His goodness, which remains forever true.
**A shepherd for His people.**

ANGEL #6

Behold, cry the angels, bringing great news of joy
Born in Bethlehem, the promised baby boy.
Now wrapped as a babe, in wisdom He'll grow
Till someday He'll gather His own.
**A shepherd for His people.**

BOBBY: "And suddenly there was with the angel a multitude of the heavenly host, praising God, and saying,"

ALL ANGELS: "Glory to God in the highest, and on earth peace, good will toward men!"

*The children in the Primary and Junior departments sing "Angels' Chorus."*

# Angels' Chorus

BOBBY: After the shepherds had seen the baby Lord Jesus, they left the manger and shared the good news of His birth with others.

*The children in the Junior and Primary departments sing "Christmas Song."*

# Christmas Song

Based on Robert Schumann's
"Happy Farmer"

Jeffery G. La

23
He so loved the world He gave His on - ly Son, all: That Christ - mas
28
morn, when Je - sus Christ was born. boys: Let's share our song, a
33
2nd time to Coda
song for ev - ery - one— girls: A song for all the world to sing, a song of
38
joy! all: It's a song of cel - e - bra - tion, for a Sa - vior of all na - tions is

born this day in Beth-le-hem. Come as we now
wor-ship the Babe born as our Sav-ior, Who sleeps this night in a man-ge
stall. Come as we now wor-ship the Babe born as our Sav-ior, Wh
sleeps this night in a man-ger stall. joy!
D.C. al Coda
Coda
© 1993, Jeffery G. La

*The children from the Primary and Junior departments exit.*

JESSICA: The first soft notes of the sweet song began to grow as the news of the Savior's birth spread.

BOBBY: The melody began in a simple stable; then it grew in the shepherds' hearts.

JESSICA: But the song did not end with the shepherds. Many people must have rejoiced when the shepherds told others what they had seen and heard. Others joined in. . . . Simeon, a devout man, and Anna, a prophetess. Later, in their hearts, the wise men undoubtedly added their own verse of this very special song. A simple song shared in a stable soon swelled to the grand symphony of God. The music of the manger became the symphony of celebration.

BOBBY: That music was the song of salvation.

JESSICA: The music of the manger that began so long ago continues today—louder than ever.

BOBBY: Sung around the world—

JESSICA: —By every nation and tongue.

BOBBY *(speaking to the audience):* Can you hear that song? the song of Christmas? a song of love? Is the song of salvation the anthem of your heart?

JESSICA: Let your heart listen to the melody of the simple truth of salvation, while your spirit listens to the lyrics of love.

*JESSICA and BOBBY exit. Scene fades to black.*

## Scene Four

*The four young people are in the living room, preparing to go caroling.*

TIM: That night—that first Christmas night was special.

BOBBY: So special that music must have been a part of the celebration. Maybe not the Christmas carols we sing. They may not have had an orchestra or band—

JESSICA: —Or even a piano.

JANICE: Perhaps they could hear the music only with their hearts.

TIM: But the shepherds heard it.

BOBBY: And they rejoiced and celebrated the birth of the Christ Child.

JESSICA: But that night, the people of Bethlehem didn't hear the angels' music, like the shepherds did.

JANICE: Maybe they weren't listening with their hearts. They probably had their hearts set on other things. They were too busy to worship the Lord Jesus.

TIM: How sad to miss the joy of Christmas. *Nobody* can be that busy.

BOBBY: Speaking of busy . . . we're so busy talking, we're missing out on singing.

JESSICA: I hope the people have time to listen to our songs about Jesus.

JANICE: I am sure our friends and neighbors will take time to listen to us. No matter how busy they are, they'll stop to listen when they find four kids like us on their doorstep, sharing our Christmas joy!

TIM: That's right. We'll sing our song, and our neighbors will listen. We'll slow them down. We'll take a few minutes out of their busy schedule to help them consider the words and music of Christmas.

JESSICA: The chance to sing of our Savior's birth is one of the greatest joys of Christmas.

BOBBY: Even better than eating cookies!

JESSICA: I know one thing for sure.

BOBBY: What's that?

JESSICA: No one will hear our songs of celebration if we don't sing them. Come on, everyone, let's get going.

TIM: We don't want to miss our chance to sing.

JANICE: If we do miss it, then we'll have to sing, "It came—and went—on a midnight clear."

BOBBY: And then tonight would be just another "silent night!"

TIM: "So come on, all ye faithful," let's go share the music of the manger.

JESSICA: Better yet, let's tell them the good news of the gospel. Let's tell our "joy to the world!"

*The four actors exit as musicians play (or the congregation sings) "Joy to the World."*

*Fade to black.*

## Epilogue

*All department and cast members return to the stage. The actors (JESSICA, BOBBY, TIM and JANICE) and/or other narrators should stand in front of the rest of the cast.*

*Participants should memorize this portion of the script and present it in a heartfelt way.*

JESSICA (OR OPTIONAL SPEAKER): Although this is the end of our Christmas play, this is not the end of the story.

BOBBY: Nor is it the end of the song.

TIM: You see, the music of the manger was only the first verse of the greatest song ever written—

JANICE: —Written by God, Himself.

TIM: The Christmas story is only the first chapter of the most amazing story.

BOBBY: We can't end the story with Christ in the cradle. For this Babe grew up to become our Savior.

JESSICA: God sent His Son to be the Savior of the world.

*Group recites John 3:16.*

JANICE: The story still isn't over.

TIM: It didn't end when Christ died on the cross.

BOBBY: For He rose from the grave on the third day, "according to the Scriptures."

JESSICA: He rose from the grave to give us victory over death—

TIM, JESSICA *(in unison):* —That we could live forevermore!

BOBBY, JANICE *(in unison):* —That we could sing His praise forever!

*If speakers are miked, music may begin to play softly in the background.*

TIM: The story will not end until Christ returns as Lord and King!

JESSICA: It's a story without end—

JANICE: —A song without end.

BOBBY: An unfinished symphony!

JESSICA: We pray that you, too, will be part of the heavenly chorus singing a symphony of praise!

*Entire cast sings "Unfinished Symphony."*

# Unfinished Symphony

Jeffery G. Lahr

30
life we might live— A song of hope, a song of love,
fin - ish the song. His reign shall be a sweet har - mo - ny—
36
writ - ten by God up a - bove. It's the mu - sic of the man - ger, The
Sweet - er than ev - er - y song. We shall sing all of our prais - es thru
42
song of our hearts. Sing al - le - lu - ia to the Lamb! It's the
e - tern - i - ty. It's the
48
mu - sic of the man - ger, The song of our hearts. Sing - ing songs of
un - fin - ished sym - pho - ny, A song with - out end.
53
1
2
prais - es to God.
God. Sing - ing songs of prais - es to God.
© 1993, Jeffery G. Lahr

JANICE,
JESSICA,
BOBBY, TIM *(in unison):* Let the song of Christmas *(slight pause)* ring in your hearts!

ALL
PARTICIPANTS: Merry Christmas, everyone!

THE END